THE PRAYER THAT Changes Everything™

Prayer and Praise Journey

STORMIE OMARTIAN

HARVEST HOUSE PUBLISHERS

EUGENE, OREGON

Cover by Koechel Peterson & Associates, Inc., Minneapolis, Minnesota

THE PRAYER THAT CHANGES EVERYTHING is a series trademark of The Hawkins Children's LLC. Harvest House Publishers, Inc., is the exclusive licensee of the trademark THE PRAYER THAT CHANGES EVERYTHING.

THE PRAYER THAT CHANGES EVERYTHING™ PRAYER AND PRAISE JOURNEY
Copyright © 2005 by Stormie Omartian
Published by Harvest House Publishers
Eugene, Oregon 97402
www.harvesthousepublishers.com

ISBN 0-7369-0194-9

Welcome to a
Life of Prayer...

No matter whether I am in the darkest and most difficult time in my life, or in a period of rest, happiness, and peace, I have learned to make worship and praise my *first* reaction to things that happen and not a last resort. Making worship and praise a personal *lifestyle* transformed my life. I want you to have that same experience.

As you answer the questions in this journal, you will be inspired with countless reasons to praise God in the midst of whatever situation you find yourself. You will be reminded to praise God during times you might not otherwise think to do so. As you write out your praise to God, you will begin to see changes happen. That's because God inhabits the praises of His people.

When we worship Him, we have a renewed sense of His presence. Praising God glorifies Him and invites His presence to invade our lives and circumstances in a powerful way. When we are in His presence, things do not remain the same. Your written praise will become a permanent record of your encounters with God and the changes He will bring about for you. You will see your praise become the prayer that changes everything in your life.

—Stormie Omartian

Because He Is
My Heavenly Father

Look at the birds of the air, for they neither sow nor reap nor gather into barns; yet your heavenly Father feeds them. Are you not of more value than they?

—Matthew 6:26

How would you describe your relationship with your earthly father? For example, was it close or distant or somewhere in between? Was it loving or abusive or somewhere in the middle? How does the relationship you had with your dad make you feel today?

_____

_____

_____

_____

_____

_____

_____

_____

_____

_____

_____

_____

_____

_____

_____

_____

What do you feel was most lacking in your relationship with your earthly father? Describe it in a prayer to the Lord and ask Him to fill in what has been missing in your life because of it. If there was nothing lacking in your relationship with your earthly father, write out a prayer of praise and thanksgiving to God for the fact that your earthly father was everything you needed him to be.

List the greatest attributes of your earthly father. If you never knew him, or barely knew him, list the attributes you would have most desired in a father. What names and attributes of God most correspond to those you have listed? Do you believe that your Father God can be all that to you now?

_____

_____

_____

_____

_____

_____

_____

_____

_____

_____

_____

_____

_____

_____

_____

_____

_____

Write out a prayer of praise thanking God that He is your heavenly Father. Ask the Lord to show you any place where you have put something on Him that was really due to a failing on the part of your earthly father.

_____

_____

_____

_____

_____

_____

_____

_____

_____

_____

_____

_____

_____

_____

_____

_____

_____

While God's love for you as His child is unconditional, He still has rules and requirements as any good parent would for their children. What are the requirements stated in 2 Corinthians 6:17-18? What are the promises?

_____

_____

_____

_____

_____

_____

_____

_____

_____

_____

_____

_____

_____

_____

_____

_____

_____

_____

Because He Loves Me

We have known and believed the love that God has for us. God is love, and he who abides in love abides in God, and God in him.

—1 JOHN 4:16

*A*re you convinced that God is a God of love? Do you feel God loves you as much as anyone else in the world? Why or why not?

_____

_____

_____

_____

_____

_____

_____

_____

_____

_____

_____

_____

_____

_____

_____

_____

_____

_____

According to 1 Corinthians 13:1-3, what happens to us when we don't have the love of God in us and flowing through us?

_____

_____

_____

_____

_____

_____

_____

_____

_____

_____

_____

_____

_____

_____

_____

_____

Take a few moments to read Jeremiah 31:3. How long will God love us? How has He drawn us to Himself? Write out your answer as a praise to God. (For example, "Lord, I praise You for Your love and that it is...")

_____

_____

_____

_____

_____

_____

_____

_____

_____

_____

_____

_____

_____

_____

_____

_____

_____

According to Ephesians 2:4-7, why does God show us mercy?

_____

_____

_____

_____

_____

_____

_____

_____

_____

_____

_____

_____

_____

_____

_____

_____

_____

_____

In light of Romans 5:5, why should we never lose hope? How do we receive God's love in our hearts?

_____

_____

_____

_____

_____

_____

_____

_____

_____

_____

_____

_____

_____

_____

_____

_____

_____

_____

_____

Because He Laid Down His Life for Me

God demonstrates His own love toward us, in that while we were still sinners, Christ died for us. Much more then, having now been justified by His blood, we shall be saved from wrath through Him.

—ROMANS 5:8-9

Take a few moments to read Ephesians 1:3-6, and then write out these verses in your own words as a praise to God for all the things contained in them for which you are thankful.

_____

_____

_____

_____

_____

_____

_____

_____

_____

_____

_____

_____

_____

_____

_____

_____

According to Ephesians 2:4-7, how did God prove His love for you?

Let Ephesians 5:2 speak to your heart today. What are we supposed to do? Why should we be motivated to do that?

_____

_____

_____

_____

_____

_____

_____

_____

_____

_____

_____

_____

_____

_____

_____

_____

_____

_____

Why did Jesus suffer? Read 1 Peter 3:18, and then write out a prayer of praise thanking Jesus for all He has done for you. Ask Him to reveal aspects of what He accomplished on the cross that you are not even fully aware of yet.

_____

_____

_____

_____

_____

_____

_____

_____

_____

_____

_____

_____

_____

_____

_____

_____

What have we been given through Jesus? What are the reasons for praising Him in Romans 5:1-2? Write out your answer as a prayer of praise to God.

_____

_____

_____

_____

_____

_____

_____

_____

_____

_____

_____

_____

_____

_____

_____

_____

_____

_____

_____

Because He Has Forgiven Me

If we confess our sins, He is faithful and just to forgive us our sins and to cleanse us from all unrighteousness.

—1 John 1:9

How much does God forgive us? Do you believe you are completely forgiven or do you struggle with guilt over something? Read Psalm 103:12 and let its message of comfort touch your heart.

_____

_____

_____

_____

_____

_____

_____

_____

_____

_____

_____

_____

_____

_____

_____

Are there any areas in your life where you feel you specifically need to be forgiven by God? If so, write them out as a confession to Him and praise Him for His forgiveness.

_____

_____

_____

_____

_____

_____

_____

_____

_____

_____

_____

_____

_____

_____

_____

_____

_____

What does Acts 2:38-39 tell us to do? What will happen when we do it? Who is included in this?

_____

_____

_____

_____

_____

_____

_____

_____

_____

_____

_____

_____

_____

_____

_____

_____

Write out a prayer of praise and worship to God for forgiving you. Tell Him what His forgiveness means to you specifically. What have you been forgiven of that makes you most grateful?

_____

_____

_____

_____

_____

_____

_____

_____

_____

_____

_____

_____

_____

_____

_____

_____

_____

_____

_____

_____

_____

Why do we have the privilege of being forgiven? Read Ephesians 1:7-8. Who deserves our praise and why?

_____

_____

_____

_____

_____

_____

_____

_____

_____

_____

_____

_____

_____

_____

_____

_____

_____

_____

_____

_____

Because He Has Given Me His Holy Spirit

Now hope does not disappoint, because the love of God has been poured out in our hearts by the Holy Spirit who was given to us.

—ROMANS 5:5

Take a few moments to think about the Holy Spirit. What do you feel are the most important elements He brings into your life? What aspects of the Holy Spirit's work do you most need and appreciate?

The Bible tells us in 1 Corinthians 3:16 and 1 Corinthians 6:19 that our body is a temple the Holy Spirit resides in. Knowing that He is as close as your heartbeat, what would you most like to receive from Him right now? (For example, "I need the Holy Spirit's guidance" or "I need to see more of the power of the Holy Spirit working in my life.") Write out a prayer asking Him for what you need.

_____

_____

_____

_____

_____

_____

_____

_____

_____

_____

_____

_____

_____

According to Romans 8:14, what is an important indication that you are a child of God? In what ways have you felt led by the Spirit of God?

_____

_____

_____

_____

_____

_____

_____

_____

_____

_____

_____

_____

_____

_____

_____

_____

_____

What does 1 Corinthians 2:12-14 have to say about why have we received the Holy Spirit? Why do we need spiritual discernment in our lives?

_____

_____

_____

_____

_____

_____

_____

_____

_____

_____

_____

_____

_____

_____

_____

_____

_____

_____

Take a few moments to look at Isaiah 63:8-10. How did God show His love toward His people? What happened to make Him turn against them?

_____

_____

_____

_____

_____

_____

_____

_____

_____

_____

_____

_____

_____

_____

_____

_____

Because He Gave Me His Word

If you abide in My word, you are My disciples indeed. And you shall know the truth, and the truth shall make you free.

—JOHN 8:31-32

According to James 1:21-25, how are we supposed to respond to God's Word? What happens when we don't respond that way? What happens when we don't just *hear* the Word but we *do* it? Why is this a reason to praise God?

_____

_____

_____

_____

_____

_____

_____

_____

_____

_____

_____

_____

_____

_____

_____

_____

_____

_____

_____

_____

Abraham was a man who gave glory to God. Consider for a few moments Romans 4:20-22. What did Abraham choose to believe? How did God respond to his faith?

_____

_____

_____

_____

_____

_____

_____

_____

_____

_____

_____

_____

_____

_____

_____

_____

_____

Today read Psalm 19:7-11 and Matthew 24:35, and then write out a praise to God for all that is good about His Word as described in these verses. What you are most grateful for with regard to your life right now?

_____

_____

_____

_____

_____

_____

_____

_____

_____

_____

_____

_____

_____

_____

_____

_____

_____

_____

According to Joshua 1:8, what are we supposed to do in response to God's Word? What will happen when we do that?

_____

_____

_____

_____

_____

_____

_____

_____

_____

_____

_____

_____

_____

_____

_____

_____

What does 2 Timothy 3:16-17 tell us about how Scripture was given to us? How does it profit us? What does it accomplish in us?

_____

_____

_____

_____

_____

_____

_____

_____

_____

_____

_____

_____

_____

_____

_____

_____

_____

_____

_____

_____

_____

Because He Is a Good God

Oh, taste and see that the LORD is good; blessed is the man who trusts in Him!

—PSALM 34:8

"Oh, give thanks to the LORD, for He is good! For His mercy endures forever" (Psalm 118:1). Write out a prayer of praise to God for all the good things you see from Him in your life.

_____

_____

_____

_____

_____

_____

_____

_____

_____

_____

_____

_____

_____

_____

_____

_____

_____

Let Psalm 65:4 speak to your heart today. God chose *you*, and now you can come before Him in prayer and praise anytime you want. As a result, where can you expect to live your life? What will always satisfy your soul?

_____

_____

_____

_____

_____

_____

_____

_____

_____

_____

_____

_____

_____

_____

_____

_____

_____

Psalm 145:8-9 contains some wonderful promises for us. Write out a prayer of praise and thanksgiving to God for all the good things listed in these verses.

_____

_____

_____

_____

_____

_____

_____

_____

_____

_____

_____

_____

_____

_____

_____

_____

_____

_____

According to Psalm 31:19, for whom has God laid up His goodness? Does that include you? Give the reason for your answer.

_____

_____

_____

_____

_____

_____

_____

_____

_____

_____

_____

_____

_____

_____

_____

_____

_____

_____

_____

_____

Let Psalm 23:6 bless your heart today. How long is the mercy and goodness of the Lord extended to us? Write out a prayer of praise and thanksgiving to God for His goodness that will be manifested in your future. Thank Him that no matter what happens you can trust that He is a good God and His goodness will always be extended toward you.

Because He Is Holy

As He who called you is holy, you also be holy in all your conduct, because it is written, "Be holy, for I am holy."

—1 PETER 1:15-16

Take a look at Romans 6:6, 13, and 19. What does Paul tell us that we are *not* to do? What are we *supposed* to do?

_____

_____

_____

_____

_____

_____

_____

_____

_____

_____

_____

_____

_____

_____

_____

_____

_____

_____

According to Revelation 4:8, how much is God praised in heaven? What do you think we will be doing a lot of in eternity? Write or speak these same words of worship as a praise to God.

_____

_____

_____

_____

_____

_____

_____

_____

_____

_____

_____

_____

_____

_____

_____

_____

_____

_____

_____

_____

Turn in your Bible to Ephesians 1:4. Whom has God chosen? When did He make that decision? How are we to be before Him?

_____

_____

_____

_____

_____

_____

_____

_____

_____

_____

_____

_____

_____

_____

_____

_____

_____

_____

_____

_____

According to 2 Corinthians 7:1, what are we to cleanse ourselves from? What are we to aspire to?

_____

_____

_____

_____

_____

_____

_____

_____

_____

_____

_____

_____

_____

_____

_____

_____

_____

_____

Luke 1:74-75 has a wonderful mandate for those who believe. How are we to serve God? How long are we to serve Him?

_____

_____

_____

_____

_____

_____

_____

_____

_____

_____

_____

_____

_____

_____

_____

_____

_____

Because He Is All-Powerful

Behold, I am the LORD, the God of all flesh. Is there anything too hard for Me?

—JEREMIAH 32:27

Is there a situation in your life now where you know you cannot do what needs to be done without the miraculous intervening power of God? Explain it in a prayer to God and ask Him to move in power on your behalf.

_____

_____

_____

_____

_____

_____

_____

_____

_____

_____

_____

_____

_____

_____

_____

_____

Can you recall a time in your life when God moved powerfully? Describe it in a prayer of praise to Him.

Take comfort in Isaiah 40:28-31 today. Describe in a prayer of praise everything in these verses which inspire hope that God will give you the power you need for your life.

_____

_____

_____

_____

_____

_____

_____

_____

_____

_____

_____

_____

_____

_____

_____

Consider the words of Jeremiah 5:22. What should the awesomeness of God's power cause us to do?

_____

_____

_____

_____

_____

_____

_____

_____

_____

_____

_____

_____

_____

_____

_____

_____

What is your greatest dream, no matter how impossible it seems? Write it out as a prayer to God and tell Him you know He is powerful enough to make that happen. Then praise Him for it and release it into His hands saying, "Nevertheless, not my will, but Yours be done."

_____

_____

_____

_____

_____

_____

_____

_____

_____

_____

_____

_____

_____

_____

_____

_____

_____

Because He Is with Me

He Himself has said, "I will never leave you nor forsake you."

—HEBREWS 13:5

According to 1 Kings 8:22-23, how does Solomon begin his prayer dedicating the temple to the Lord? What does he say about God?

_____

_____

_____

_____

_____

_____

_____

_____

_____

_____

_____

_____

_____

_____

_____

_____

_____

What is the greatest longing of your heart? Write it out in detail as a prayer to God, and then praise Him for all the ways His presence meets that need.

_____

_____

_____

_____

_____

_____

_____

_____

_____

_____

_____

_____

_____

_____

_____

_____

_____

_____

_____

In Psalm 27:4, David says, "One thing I have desired of the LORD, that will I seek..." What is the one thing you desire of the Lord? Write it out as a prayer to Him.

_____

_____

_____

_____

_____

_____

_____

_____

_____

_____

_____

_____

_____

_____

_____

_____

_____

_____

_____

Have you been able to lay your heart bare before the Lord? Have you been able to reveal all aspects of how you feel to Him? If not, tell Him now. If you have, tell Him again.

Take a few moments to write out a prayer of praise for God's presence in your life. Enjoy telling Him all the ways you worship Him.

_____

_____

_____

_____

_____

_____

_____

_____

_____

_____

_____

_____

_____

_____

_____

_____

_____

_____

Because He Has a Purpose for My Life

We are His workmanship, created in Christ Jesus for good works, which God prepared beforehand that we should walk in them.

—EPHESIANS 2:10

According to Romans 12:1, what is the first step you must take in your service for the Lord so that you can begin to understand your purpose?

_____

_____

_____

_____

_____

_____

_____

_____

_____

_____

_____

_____

_____

_____

_____

_____

_____

What does 2 Timothy 1:9 have to say about God's calling on your life? Is it because of something you have done? If not, why has He called you?

_____

_____

_____

_____

_____

_____

_____

_____

_____

_____

_____

_____

_____

_____

_____

_____

_____

_____

_____

According to 2 Thessalonians 1:11, how should you pray with regard to your calling?

_____

_____

_____

_____

_____

_____

_____

_____

_____

_____

_____

_____

_____

_____

_____

_____

_____

_____

What is Psalm 90:17 a prayer for? Write this verse out in your own words as a prayer to God for the work you do or *want* to do. Include praise for the purpose God has for your life in the work you do and *will* do in the future.

_____

_____

_____

_____

_____

_____

_____

_____

_____

_____

_____

_____

_____

_____

_____

_____

_____

_____

_____

"As each one has received a gift, minister it to one another, as good stewards of the manifold grace of God" (1 Peter 4:10). What gifts do you have that would be a blessing to others? How could you use the gifts God has given you in your ministry or work? Write your answer out as a prayer asking God for that to happen, and then praise Him that He has a purpose for your life and gifts and will use them for His glory.

_____

_____

_____

_____

_____

_____

_____

_____

_____

_____

_____

_____

_____

_____

_____

_____

Because He Redeems All Things

They remembered that God was their rock, and the Most High God their Redeemer.

—PSALM 78:35

According to Titus 2:11-14, how does God want us to live? Why did Jesus sacrifice Himself for us?

_____

_____

_____

_____

_____

_____

_____

_____

_____

_____

_____

_____

_____

_____

_____

_____

_____

_____

_____

Spend a few moments today with Galatians 4:4-5. Why did Jesus come? What can we become because of His redemption?

_____

_____

_____

_____

_____

_____

_____

_____

_____

_____

_____

_____

_____

_____

_____

_____

_____

_____

_____

According to Psalm 103:4, from what does God redeem our lives? Write out a prayer of praise to Him listing all the reasons to praise Him in this verse.

_____

_____

_____

_____

_____

_____

_____

_____

_____

_____

_____

_____

_____

_____

_____

_____

_____

_____

_____

_____

What does Psalm 130:7 say about where should we put our hope? Why should we put our hope there?

According to Colossians 1:13-14, in whom do we have redemption? How did we get it? From what has He set us free?

_____

_____

_____

_____

_____

_____

_____

_____

_____

_____

_____

_____

_____

_____

_____

_____

_____

_____

Because He Is the Light of the World

I am the light of the world. He who follows Me shall not walk in darkness, but have the light of life.

—JOHN 8:12

According to Exodus 34:29-30, why did Moses' face shine so brightly? Who had he been with? Who noticed his radiance? What was it a reflection of?

_____

_____

_____

_____

_____

_____

_____

_____

_____

_____

_____

_____

_____

_____

_____

_____

_____

After reading Revelation 22:4-5, take a moment to explain why we will we not need light from the sun in heaven.

_____

_____

_____

_____

_____

_____

_____

_____

_____

_____

_____

_____

_____

_____

_____

_____

_____

_____

_____

_____

_____

According to 1 John 1:5-7, is there any darkness in God? If we say we are in God but continue to walk in darkness, what does that say about us? What do we have to do to have fellowship with one another?

_____

_____

_____

_____

_____

_____

_____

_____

_____

_____

_____

_____

_____

_____

_____

_____

Take a look at Revelation 21:23, which describes for us the power of God's glory. Why did the city have no need of light? Write out a praise to God telling Him how thankful you are that because of His presence in your life, you need not be afraid of the dark.

_____

_____

_____

_____

_____

_____

_____

_____

_____

_____

_____

_____

_____

_____

_____

_____

_____

_____

According to Daniel 5:13-14, what had the king heard about Daniel? Write out a prayer to God asking that those same qualities be seen in you by those around you.

_____

_____

_____

_____

_____

_____

_____

_____

_____

_____

_____

_____

_____

_____

_____

_____

_____

_____

_____

_____

_____

Because He Is

You are worthy, O Lord, to receive glory and honor and power; for You created all things, and by Your will they exist and were created.

—REVELATION 4:11

Revelation 21:6 has a wonderful promise for us. Who is God in this verse? What will He give to you when you long for His presence?

_____

_____

_____

_____

_____

_____

_____

_____

_____

_____

_____

_____

_____

_____

_____

_____

_____

_____

According to Psalm 14:2, what is the Lord looking for? What can you do to be what God wants?

_____

_____

_____

_____

_____

_____

_____

_____

_____

_____

_____

_____

_____

_____

_____

_____

Have you ever just gone before the Lord and sat in His presence and simply worshiped Him? If so, describe what that was like. If not, write out a prayer asking God to help you do that often.

_____

_____

_____

_____

_____

_____

_____

_____

_____

_____

_____

_____

_____

_____

_____

_____

_____

"Come to Me, all you who labor and are heavy laden, and I will give you rest" (Matthew 11:28). What happens when we simply come to God?

Why are we to worship God? Read Psalm 45:11, and then write out a prayer of praise to God, thanking Him for simply being in your life and living in your heart.

_____

_____

_____

_____

_____

_____

_____

_____

_____

_____

_____

_____

_____

_____

_____

_____

When I Am Troubled by Negative Thoughts and Emotions

Be anxious for nothing, but in everything by prayer and supplication, with thanksgiving, let your requests be made known to God; and the peace of God, which surpasses all understanding, will guard your hearts and minds through Christ Jesus. Finally, brethren, whatever things are true, whatever things are noble, whatever things are just, whatever things are pure, whatever things are lovely, whatever things are of good report, if there is any virtue and if there is anything praiseworthy—meditate on these things.

—PHILIPPIANS 4:6-8

*W*hat did Jesus come to earth to do for His people? Take a look at Isaiah 61:1-3 and how Jesus fulfilled these verses. Whom did He come to comfort? What will He give them? Write out a prayer of praise to God for all the things listed in these verses for which you are grateful. Describe what you are *most* thankful for, especially with regard to any negative emotions you may be feeling or have felt. (For example, "Lord, I praise You and thank You that You came to earth to heal those who are brokenhearted...")

According to Psalm 9:9-10, what can we do when we feel oppressed with negative emotions? What will happen when we do that?

_____

_____

_____

_____

_____

_____

_____

_____

_____

_____

_____

_____

_____

_____

_____

_____

Do you have any negative thoughts and emotions troubling you right now? How long have you had them? Have you ever accepted those kinds of thoughts and feelings as "just the way you are"? Write out a prayer below giving those emotions and thoughts to God. Ask Him to set you free from them and give you His thoughts.

_____

_____

_____

_____

_____

_____

_____

_____

_____

_____

_____

_____

_____

_____

_____

_____

_____

_____

_____

_____

_____

What does Hebrews 4:12 have to say about how the Word of God can help us in our thinking and feelings?

_____

_____

_____

_____

_____

_____

_____

_____

_____

_____

_____

_____

_____

_____

_____

_____

According to Philippians 4:8, what are we supposed to think about instead of negative things? Write your answer out as a prayer to God and praise Him for His answer and His Word. (For example, "Lord, I pray that You would help me to think only thoughts that are true...")

_____

_____

_____

_____

_____

_____

_____

_____

_____

_____

_____

_____

_____

_____

_____

_____

_____

When I Have Anxiety, Fear, and Discouragement

God is our refuge and strength, a very present help in trouble.
Therefore we will not fear, even though the earth be removed,
and though the mountains be carried into the midst of the sea.

—Psalm 46:1-2

What are the things you fear most right now? What attributes of God are you most grateful for with regard to the things you fear most? Write your answer out as a praise to God.

_____

_____

_____

_____

_____

_____

_____

_____

_____

_____

_____

_____

_____

_____

_____

_____

_____

_____

Take a few moments to read John 6:18-21. Why were the disciples afraid? What did Jesus tell them that comforted them? How did the disciples respond to Him? What happened immediately after that? Do you think that by receiving Jesus into your own circumstances it would calm your fears and get you safely to where you need to go too?

According to Psalm 34:1-10, how much and how often are we to praise God? What does it do for others when they see us praising God in the midst of our fear? Write out a prayer of praise for the things you are thankful for in this section of Scripture.

The psalms are rich with examples of the Lord hearing those who cry out to Him for help. Take a few moments to read Psalm 34:17-22, and then write out a prayer of praise to God for all that you are thankful for in these verses, especially with regard to your life right now.

Psalm 103 is a wonderful example of a heart that is grateful for the merciful love of the Lord. Write out a prayer of praise to God for all that you are thankful for in this psalm.

_____

_____

_____

_____

_____

_____

_____

_____

_____

_____

_____

_____

_____

_____

_____

_____

_____

_____

_____

_____

_____

When I Become Sick, Weak, or Injured

He was wounded for our transgressions, He was bruised for our iniquities; the chastisement for our peace was upon Him, and by His stripes we are healed.

—Isaiah 53:5

"For we know that if our earthly house, this tent, is destroyed, we have a building from God, a house not made with hands, eternal in the heavens" (2 Corinthians 5:1). What is our ultimate hope when we are not healed as we prayed?

_____

_____

_____

_____

_____

_____

_____

_____

_____

_____

_____

_____

_____

_____

_____

_____

_____

_____

_____

According to Isaiah 58:6-12, what are some of the things that can happen when we observe the fast God has chosen and pray?

_____

_____

_____

_____

_____

_____

_____

_____

_____

_____

_____

_____

_____

_____

_____

_____

_____

_____

Take a look at Psalm 102:1-12, which is a prayer David lifted up when he was afflicted and overwhelmed with his condition. What did he do in the midst of it?

_____

_____

_____

_____

_____

_____

_____

_____

_____

_____

_____

_____

_____

_____

_____

_____

_____

_____

Think for a moment again about Psalm 102:1-12. Have you ever felt the way David did? Do you feel that way now? What can you praise God for in the midst of your suffering?

_____

_____

_____

_____

_____

_____

_____

_____

_____

_____

_____

_____

_____

_____

_____

_____

_____

_____

What are the promises of God in Exodus 15:26 and Jeremiah 30:17? How do they give you hope?

_____

_____

_____

_____

_____

_____

_____

_____

_____

_____

_____

_____

_____

_____

_____

When I Struggle with Doubts

Faith comes by hearing, and hearing by the word of God.

—ROMANS 10:17

According to James 1:6-8, how are we to ask for things from God? What happens when we allow doubt to be part of our lives?

I Believe — I Just believe —
All — EVERy thing — I Will
Not Waiver! You are the
King — I am not — You know
My hearts desires — my sweet
feelings, for Myself for
My Life + ministry — Your
timing Lord — I believe —
I look to you and ask
For All you desire for me
to be done — it is All you —
I give All up for you. Amen!

"Now the just shall live by faith; but if anyone draws back, my soul has no pleasure in him" (Hebrews 10:38). How are we supposed to live? What happens when we don't?

_____

_____

_____

_____

_____

_____

_____

_____

_____

_____

_____

_____

_____

_____

_____

_____

_____

_____

_____

_____

_____

Has anything happened to you recently or in the past that has caused you to feel doubt about God's ability or desire to help you and take care of you? Do you truly believe that God always has your best interests in mind?

*I*n what area is your faith weakest? Write it out as a prayer of confession to the Lord. (For example, "Lord, I confess that my faith is weakest when it comes to my finances...") Then write out a prayer of worship, praise, and thanksgiving to God for the things about Him that most encourage you in this area where your faith is weakest. (For example, "Lord, I praise You that You are my Provider. Thank You that You are a God of restoration and blessing...")

Take a look at Hebrews 11 with your own life of faith in mind.
What of the things these great people did by faith do you most
want to emulate? (For example, "I would like to have the faith to
follow God wherever He leads me the way Abraham did men-
tioned in verse 8.")

_____

_____

_____

_____

_____

_____

_____

_____

_____

_____

_____

_____

_____

_____

_____

_____

_____

When I Don't See Answers to My Prayers

The LORD is good to those who wait for Him, to the soul who seeks Him.

—LAMENTATIONS 3:25

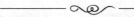

Is there anything you have been praying about for quite some time that you have not seen an answer to yet? How do you feel about that? Are you discouraged or hopeful? Write it out as a prayer. (For example, "Lord, I lift up my marriage to You again and ask You to heal it and make it good and solid…")

_____

_____

_____

_____

_____

_____

_____

_____

_____

_____

_____

_____

_____

Write out a prayer of praise and worship to God for the things about Him that most pertain to your greatest needs. Tell Him what it is about Him that inspires you to trust Him to answer in His way and His time. (For example, "Lord, I praise You that You are a God of love, redemption, forgiveness, and restoration...")

What do you know about God that gives you the most peace regarding what you have been praying about?

_____

_____

_____

_____

_____

_____

_____

_____

_____

_____

_____

_____

_____

_____

_____

_____

_____

"Let us hold fast the confession of our hope without wavering, for He who promised is faithful" (Hebrews 10:23). What should you do while waiting for God to answer your prayer?

_____

_____

_____

_____

_____

_____

_____

_____

_____

_____

_____

_____

_____

_____

_____

_____

_____

_____

_____

_____

According to Psalm 13, what did David say to the Lord about his struggle with unanswered prayer? Even though his prayers were not answered, what did he do? Write in your own words the praise David spoke to the Lord.

_____

_____

_____

_____

_____

_____

_____

_____

_____

_____

_____

_____

_____

_____

_____

_____

_____

_____

When I Have Problems in a Relationship

A new commandment I give to you, that you love one another; as I have loved you, that you also love one another.

—JOHN 13:34

After reading Ecclesiastes 4:9-12, describe in your own words why relationships are important.

How did David respond when people said bad things about him? Read Psalm 27:12-14. What kept him from losing heart? How should we respond?

_____

_____

_____

_____

_____

_____

_____

_____

_____

_____

_____

_____

_____

_____

_____

_____

_____

_____

_____

_____

According to 1 John 3:16, how are we to treat our relationships? Why? In what ways can we lay down our lives for others? (Because Jesus paid the ultimate price, John is not talking about *us* dying. He is talking about us making a sacrifice for others.)

_____

_____

_____

_____

_____

_____

_____

_____

_____

_____

_____

_____

_____

_____

_____

_____

_____

_____

Do you have a relationship in your life that is especially difficult or troubling for you right now? What is the condition of that relationship? What good seeds have you sown into that relationship in the past? (For example, "I have spent a lot of time or resources on them. I have encouraged them. I have kept in close contact with them. I have been kind and loving toward them. I have told them how much I care about them. I pray for them often...") What could you praise God for in that relationship right now?

_____

_____

_____

_____

_____

_____

_____

_____

_____

_____

_____

_____

_____

_____

_____

What good seeds could you sow into all your relationships that would make a big difference in each of them? (For example, "I could call them more often to see how they are or if they need anything. I could tell them how important they are to me. I could pray for them every day…") Write out a prayer of praise to God for those people in your life, and ask Him to fill you so full of His love that it overflows onto them.

_____

_____

_____

_____

_____

_____

_____

_____

_____

_____

_____

_____

_____

_____

_____

_____

_____

_____

_____

When I Need to Forgive

Be kind to one another, tenderhearted, forgiving one another, even as God in Christ forgave you.

—EPHESIANS 4:32

Write out a prayer praising God for all that He has forgiven you. Be specific. Praise Jesus for the tremendous price He paid to secure this forgiveness for you. Thank Him in advance for the times He will need to forgive you again in the future.

Take a few moments to read Mark 11:25-26. What is it in these verses that most inspires you to forgive?

_____

_____

_____

_____

_____

_____

_____

_____

_____

_____

_____

_____

_____

_____

_____

_____

_____

*I*s there someone in your life you need to forgive? Is it a family member or friend? Is it someone with whom you do business? Is it yourself? Is it God? Write out a prayer confessing your lack of forgiveness, and then ask God to help you forgive that person or those persons completely.

_____

_____

_____

_____

_____

_____

_____

_____

_____

_____

_____

_____

_____

_____

_____

_____

According to Matthew 22:37-39, how can we show our love for God? How can we show our love for others?

_____

_____

_____

_____

_____

_____

_____

_____

_____

_____

_____

_____

_____

_____

_____

_____

Take a look at Job 42:10. What did God do for Job when he forgave his well-meaning, but hurtful, friends?

_____

_____

_____

_____

_____

_____

_____

_____

_____

_____

_____

_____

_____

_____

_____

_____

_____

_____

_____

_____

When I See Things Going Wrong and I Feel Powerless

Be of good courage, and He shall strengthen your heart, all you who hope in the LORD.

—PSALM 31:24

According to 2 Corinthians 1:3-4, where do we find comfort during our times of trial? What is one of the purposes of these difficult times? What good can come out of it?

_____

_____

_____

_____

_____

_____

_____

_____

_____

_____

_____

_____

_____

_____

_____

_____

_____

Isaiah 41:10 contains great comfort. Why do we not need to be afraid or dismayed during a time of trial or struggle? Write out a praise to God for the promises in this Scripture.

_____

_____

_____

_____

_____

_____

_____

_____

_____

_____

_____

_____

_____

_____

_____

_____

Take a few moments to read James 1:2-4 and Ecclesiastes 7:8. Why should we find joy in the midst of our trials? Why is it important to learn to have patience? Write out a prayer asking God to help you have joy and patience in the difficult times of your life.

_____

_____

_____

_____

_____

_____

_____

_____

_____

_____

_____

_____

_____

_____

_____

_____

According to Psalm 107:28-32, what happens when we are in the middle of a storm in our lives and we cry out to God? What does God do in response? What should we do in response to Him?

_____

_____

_____

_____

_____

_____

_____

_____

_____

_____

_____

_____

_____

_____

_____

_____

"For I consider that the sufferings of this present time are not worthy to be compared with the glory which shall be revealed in us" (Romans 8:18). How are we to look at our times of suffering?

_____

_____

_____

_____

_____

_____

_____

_____

_____

_____

_____

_____

_____

_____

_____

_____

_____

When I Long to Know God's Will

We...do not cease to pray for you, and to ask that you may be filled with the knowledge of His will in all wisdom and spiritual understanding; that you may walk worthy of the Lord, fully pleasing Him, being fruitful in every good work and increasing in the knowledge of God.

—COLOSSIANS 1:9-10

According to Isaiah 30:21, what are we supposed to do to find God's will? Write out a prayer of praise and thanksgiving for the promise in this Scripture for you.

_____

_____

_____

_____

_____

_____

_____

_____

_____

_____

_____

_____

_____

_____

_____

_____

_____

Realizing the perfect will of God in our lives is linked to what, according to Romans 12:2?

_____

_____

_____

_____

_____

_____

_____

_____

_____

_____

_____

_____

_____

_____

_____

_____

_____

_____

Take a few moments to read Psalm 16:7-8. Who gives us counsel? What does that guarantee you?

Do you have a decision to make soon that you must have the mind of Christ about so that you can act according to God's will? Write out a prayer to God asking Him to reveal His will to you in this matter. Be specific.

_____

_____

_____

_____

_____

_____

_____

_____

_____

_____

_____

_____

_____

_____

_____

_____

Write out a prayer to God praising Him for who He is and for His perfect will in your life. Thank Him that He is a God who makes His will known to those who seek to know it. Thank Him that He will reveal His perfect will in regard to the matters that concern you.

_____

_____

_____

_____

_____

_____

_____

_____

_____

_____

_____

_____

_____

When I Seek Breakthrough, Deliverance, or Transformation

Do not remember the former things, nor consider the things of old. Behold, I will do a new thing, now it shall spring forth; shall you not know it? I will even make a road in the wilderness and rivers in the desert.

—ISAIAH 43:18-19

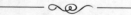

"Nevertheless He saved them for His name's sake, that He might make His mighty power known" (Psalm 106:8). Why does God deliver or rescue us?

_____

_____

_____

_____

_____

_____

_____

_____

_____

_____

_____

_____

_____

_____

_____

_____

_____

_____

_____

_____

Read John 16:33 and then explain how this verse can encourage you in your need for breakthrough and deliverance.

_____

_____

_____

_____

_____

_____

_____

_____

_____

_____

_____

_____

_____

_____

_____

_____

_____

According to Luke 4:18-19, what has God promised to do for you, and how does this encourage you in believing you can break through all barriers in your life and find freedom and deliverance?

_____

_____

_____

_____

_____

_____

_____

_____

_____

_____

_____

_____

_____

_____

_____

_____

_____

In Isaiah 58:6, God describes the fast He Himself has chosen. What does this particular fast accomplish?

What are the promises of God to you in Psalm 91:15-16 with regard to seeing breakthrough and deliverance in your life?

_____

_____

_____

_____

_____

_____

_____

_____

_____

_____

_____

_____

_____

_____

_____

_____

_____

_____

_____

_____

When I Need God's Provision and Protection

The LORD is my shepherd; I shall not want. He makes me to lie down in green pastures; He leads me beside the still waters. He restores my soul; He leads me in the paths of righteousness for His name's sake. Yea, though I walk through the valley of the shadow of death, I will fear no evil; for You are with me; Your rod and Your staff, they comfort me. You prepare a table before me in the presence of my enemies; You anoint my head with oil; my cup runs over. Surely goodness and mercy shall follow me all the days of my life; and I will dwell in the house of the LORD forever.

—PSALM 23

Take a few moments to look at James 1:17, and then write out a prayer of praise to God as Lord over your life, thanking Him that He is your Provider and Protector. Thank Him for all He has provided for you in the past, is providing for you now, and will provide for you in the future. Ask Him to show you if you have been a good steward of all He has given you.

In Luke 6:38 we are given some instruction on giving. What are we supposed to do? What will happen when we do that? Write out a prayer of praise to God, thanking Him for this promise.

_____

_____

_____

_____

_____

_____

_____

_____

_____

_____

_____

_____

_____

_____

_____

_____

_____

_____

_____

Faithful stewardship is a way we can honor the Lord. According to Malachi 3:10, what is required of us? What will God do for us when we do that?

_____

_____

_____

_____

_____

_____

_____

_____

_____

_____

_____

_____

_____

_____

_____

Take a few moments to consider Proverbs 21:13 and Psalm 41:1-2. According to these verses, what are we to do? What happens if we don't? What happens if we do?

_____

_____

_____

_____

_____

_____

_____

_____

_____

_____

_____

_____

_____

_____

_____

_____

_____

"For where your treasure is, there your heart will be also" (Matthew 6:21). Write out a prayer of worship and praise to God telling Him how much you reverence Him. Proclaim Him as your most valuable treasure.

_____

_____

_____

_____

_____

_____

_____

_____

_____

_____

_____

_____

_____

_____

_____

_____

_____

_____

When I Fight Temptation to Walk in the Flesh

Those who live according to the flesh set their minds on the things of the flesh, but those who live according to the Spirit, the things of the Spirit.

—ROMANS 8:5

According to James 1:12-15, what happens when you endure temptation and don't give in to it? What has God promised? Does God tempt us? How are we tempted?

_____

_____

_____

_____

_____

_____

_____

_____

_____

_____

_____

_____

_____

_____

_____

_____

_____

The patience of the Lord is often more than we deserve. Take a few moments to read Psalm 103:8-9. What should we praise God for in these verses? Write out your own prayer of praise to God.

According to Luke 6:46-49, what does being obedient to God do for our lives? How does our obedience protect us? If we don't obey, what does that do to our relationship with Him?

_____

_____

_____

_____

_____

_____

_____

_____

_____

_____

_____

_____

_____

_____

_____

_____

_____

_____

How is God faithful when we are tempted to do wrong? Take a few moments to read 1 Corinthians 10:13 and then write your answer out as a prayer of praise to God, thanking Him for all that.

_____

_____

_____

_____

_____

_____

_____

_____

_____

_____

_____

_____

_____

_____

_____

_____

_____

_____

According to Romans 8:12-17, what happens when we live according to the flesh? What should we do in order to live? What do we become if we are led by the Spirit?

_____

_____

_____

_____

_____

_____

_____

_____

_____

_____

_____

_____

_____

_____

_____

_____

_____

_____

When I Am Attacked by the Enemy

He sent from above, He took me; He drew me out of many waters. He delivered me from my strong enemy, from those who hated me, for they were too strong for me. They confronted me in the day of my calamity, but the LORD was my support. He also brought me out into a broad place; He delivered me because He delighted in me.

—PSALM 18:16-19

David knew what it was like to be surrounded by his enemies. Take a few moments to read Psalm 118:5-20. Which verses speak most powerfully to you about your life right now? Choose three verses that most inspire you to praise God when the enemy attacks and you are in the midst of a battle.

_____

_____

_____

_____

_____

_____

_____

_____

_____

_____

_____

_____

_____

_____

King Jehoshaphat also looked to the Lord in a time of desperate trouble. His story is found in 2 Chronicles 20:1-22. What do verses 3, 6, 9, 12, 15, 17, 18, and 21 speak to you about any difficult situation you might be going through in your life right now, or one you might face in the future? What do they inspire you to do?

_____

_____

_____

_____

_____

_____

_____

_____

_____

_____

_____

_____

_____

_____

_____

According to Psalm 44:5-8, who should you trust when the enemy of your soul rises up against you? What will God do? What are we not to trust in? What should we do for God?

_____

_____

_____

_____

_____

_____

_____

_____

_____

_____

_____

_____

_____

_____

_____

God is watching over you. Write out a prayer of praise to Him thanking Him for all the things about Him that you are grateful for with regard to fighting the battles in your life.

_____

_____

_____

_____

_____

_____

_____

_____

_____

_____

_____

_____

_____

_____

_____

_____

_____

_____

_____

_____

_____

According to 1 Peter 5:9, what are we supposed to do when the enemy attacks us? What should give us the strength and inspiration to do so?

_____

_____

_____

_____

_____

_____

_____

_____

_____

_____

_____

_____

_____

_____

_____

_____

When I Suffer Great Loss, Disappointment, or Failure

Be merciful to me, O God, be merciful to me! For my soul trusts in You; and in the shadow of Your wings I will make my refuge, until these calamities have passed by. I will cry out to God Most High, to God who performs all things for me.

—PSALM 57:1-2

David understood the pain of great loss as well as the joy of great success. Take a few moments to read 2 Samuel 12:19-20. After David's tragedy, what did he do?

_____

_____

_____

_____

_____

_____

_____

_____

_____

_____

_____

_____

_____

_____

_____

_____

_____

_____

_____

_____

What is the greatest loss you have experienced in your life? Were you able to praise God through it or in the midst of it? Why or why not?

What is the greatest disappointment you have experienced in your life? How did you survive it? How do you feel about it now? What is the promise for you in Psalm 146:8?

_____

_____

_____

_____

_____

_____

_____

_____

_____

_____

_____

_____

_____

_____

_____

_____

_____

In light of Romans 8:28, what good do you see coming out of any difficult situation you find yourself in? If you can't think of anything, write out a prayer asking God to show you the good in your situation and then lift up praise to Him for that.

Write out a prayer of praise to God thanking Him for all His specific attributes for which you are especially grateful with regard to your loss, disappointment, or failure. (For example, "Lord, I thank You that You are a God of grace and mercy and redemption...")

_____

_____

_____

_____

_____

_____

_____

_____

_____

_____

_____

_____

_____

_____

_____

_____

When I Sense that All Is Well

LORD, lift up the light of Your countenance upon us. You have put gladness in my heart, more than in the season that their grain and wine increased. I will both lie down in peace, and sleep; for You alone, O LORD, make me dwell in safety.

—PSALM 4:6-8

According to 1 Corinthians 15:58, what are we to always do, no matter what is happening? How can you apply this to your life in the good times as well as the difficult and challenging times?

_____

_____

_____

_____

_____

_____

_____

_____

_____

_____

_____

_____

_____

_____

_____

_____

_____

_____

_____

Write out a prayer asking God to help you stand strong in all you know of Him all the time. Ask Him to help you not forget to do that when things are going well.

_____

_____

_____

_____

_____

_____

_____

_____

_____

_____

_____

_____

_____

_____

_____

_____

_____

_____

Take a few moments to read 1 Thessalonians 5:16-18. What are we to do all the time, no matter what is happening? Write out a prayer asking God to help you do those things every day.

_____

_____

_____

_____

_____

_____

_____

_____

_____

_____

_____

_____

_____

_____

_____

_____

_____

Write out a prayer of praise and thanksgiving for all the good things God has brought into your life. Commit to praising Him for these things in the good times as well as the difficult.

_____

_____

_____

_____

_____

_____

_____

_____

_____

_____

_____

_____

_____

_____

_____

_____

_____

_____

_____

_____

_____

According to 1 Corinthians 16:13, what are you to do at all times? How will this help you later on if you do this in the good times?

_____

_____

_____

_____

_____

_____

_____

_____

_____

_____

_____

_____

_____

_____

_____

_____

Dear Reader,

One of the greatest things you can do for yourself and others is to put on a CD of worship music and let it play through your home, car, place of work, or wherever you spend your time. Worship music will not only change the atmosphere of where you are, but it will also change your attitude and thoughts, and give you peace of mind and joy. That's why my husband, Michael, and I put 11 of our favorite praise and worship songs together and matched them up with our favorite singers and made a CD for you to not only listen to, but to use as the perfect companion to this book.

The songs correspond to the book chapters in their content and will inspire you to a powerful time of personal praise and worship of our awesome God. Michael's beautiful arrangements and production of these songs, and the anointed voices who sing them (each singer a worship leader with a heart for worship), will stir your heart to respond. In fact, I believe they will touch you so deeply that you will find yourself singing them throughout the day, long after the CD has been played.

The name of this CD is the same as the book, *The Prayer That Changes Everything* (Integrity Music). You should be able to find it wherever the book is sold.

With many blessings,

Stormie Omartian

New Companion Worship Album

Stormie Omartian and her multi-Grammy
Award-winning husband, Michael,
have hand-selected this collection of powerful
praise and worship songs to usher us closer
to the heart of God.

———— ✑ ————

This ALL NEW recording includes favorite
worship songs plus NEW songs penned by
Stormie and her husband.

Produced by Michael, this album features various
vocalists including daughter Amanda Omartian.

OTHER BOOKS
BY STORMIE OMARTIAN

THE POWER OF A PRAYING® WOMAN
Stormie Omartian's bestselling books have helped hundreds of thousands of individuals pray more effectively for their spouses, their children, and their nation. Now she has written a book on a subject she knows intimately: being a praying woman. Stormie's deep knowledge of Scripture and candid examples from her own prayer life provide guidance for women who seek to trust God with deep longings and cover every area of life with prayer.

THE POWER OF A PRAYING® WIFE
Stormie shares how wives can develop a deeper relationship with their husbands by praying for them. With this practical advice on praying for specific areas, including decision making, fears, spiritual strength, and sexuality, women will discover the fulfilling marriage God intended.

THE POWER OF A PRAYING® HUSBAND
Building on the success of *The Power of a Praying® Wife*, Stormie offers this guide to help husbands pray more effectively for their wives. Each chapter features comments from well-known Christian men, biblical wisdom, and prayer ideas.

THE POWER OF A PRAYING® PARENT
This powerful book for parents offers 30 easy-to-read chapters that focus on specific areas of prayers for children. This personal, practical guide leads the way to enriched, strong prayer lives for both moms and dads.

THE POWER OF A PRAYING® NATION
Learn to intercede in practical ways for our political leaders, military personnel, teachers, and those who work in the media. Affect the strength and spiritual life of our nation through prayer.

THE POWER OF PRAYING™ TOGETHER (with Jack Hayford)
Stormie and her longtime pastor, Jack Hayford, look at the benefits and power of praying with others. More than just a "how to" book, *The Power of Praying™ Together* helps readers discover that when they are willing to link their hearts with others before God, they open themselves up to a wider, more interactive world of prayer.

JUST ENOUGH LIGHT FOR THE STEP I'M ON
New Christians and those experiencing life changes or difficult times will appreciate Stormie's honesty, candor, and advice based on experience and the Word of God in this collection of devotional readings perfect for the pressures of today's world.